First edition 2016

Copyright © 2016 Anno Domini Publishing
www.ad-publishing.com
Text copyright © 2016 Bethan James
Illustrations copyright © 2015 Krisztina Kállai Nagy

Published 2017 by Authentic Media Ltd
PO Box 6326, Bletchley, Milton Keynes, MK1 9GG, UK
www.authenticmedia.co.uk
ISBN: 978 1 86024 984 6
Conforms to EN71 and AS/NZS ISO 8124

Publishing Director: Annette Reynolds
Art Director: Gerald Rogers
Pre-production Manager: Doug Hewitt

Printed and bound in China

My Little Hands Bible

Bethan James and
Krisztina Kállai Nagy

Contents

In the beginning	8
Noah's ark	10
The tower of Babel	12
Abraham's big family	14
Esau and Jacob	16
Jacob tricks his father	18
Jacob's favourite son	20
Sold to be a slave	22
The king of Egypt	24
A very happy family	26
Moses and the princess	28
The king says 'No!'	30
Escape from Egypt	32
Gideon's fleece	34
A boy called Samuel	36
David and the giant	38
Elijah and the ravens	40
One more drop of oil	42
Washing in the river	44

Jonah and the big fish	46
Daniel and the lions	48
Mary and the angel	50
Mary and Elizabeth	52
Joseph the carpenter	54
The journey to Bethlehem	56
No room at the inn	58
The first Christmas	60
Shepherds on the hillside	62
The baby Jesus	64
Wise men in the east	66
Following a star	68
Bad King Herod	70
Gold, frankincense and myrrh	72
Jesus is baptised	74
Jesus chooses friends	76
A hole in the roof	78
God loves you!	80
Jesus calms a storm	82
Jesus heals a little girl	84

The boy who shared	86
The story of the kind man	88
The story of the lost sheep	90
Jesus heals a blind man	92
The man who climbed a tree	94
Mary, Martha and Lazarus	96
Jesus rides a donkey	98
Love one another	100
The last supper	102
Praying in the garden	104
Jesus on trial	106
The angry crowd	108
The heavy cross	110
Jesus is crucified	112
Buried in a rock tomb	114
Jesus is alive!	116
Jesus meets his friends	118
Thomas believes	120
Breakfast on the beach	122
The Holy Spirit comes	124

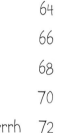

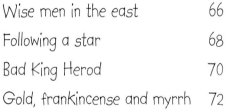
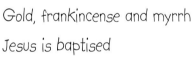
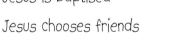
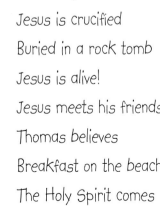

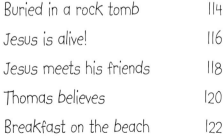

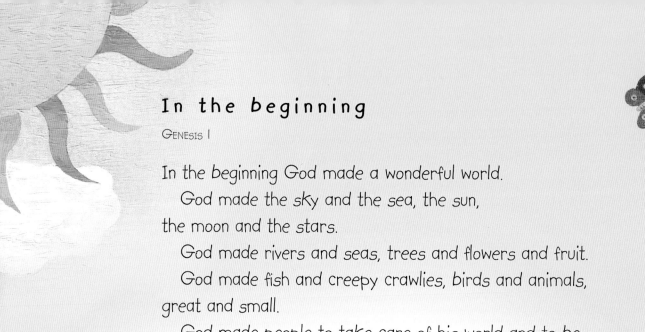

In the beginning

GENESIS 1

In the beginning God made a wonderful world.

God made the sky and the sea, the sun,
the moon and the stars.

God made rivers and seas, trees and flowers and fruit.

God made fish and creepy crawlies, birds and animals,
great and small.

God made people to take care of his world and to be
his friends.

Noah's ark

GENESIS 6 - 9

God told Noah to build a BIG boat called an ark.

Animals came from far and near and went into the ark, two by two. Then pitter-pat, pitter-pat; drip, drop, splash! It rained and it rained and it rained so that a HUGE flood destroyed the land.

God took care of Noah, his family and all the animals until it was safe to come out of the ark and to start all over again.

The tower of Babel

GENESIS 11

Noah's sons had children and grandchildren and
great grandchildren and after a time there were
very many people living again upon the earth.

'Let's build a great city,' they said. 'Let's
build a high tower so everyone can see how
great and wonderful we are!'

God saw how quickly people
had forgotten him and thought
only of themselves again. So
God confused their language.
Suddenly they couldn't
understand each other. They
stopped building the tower.
And they moved away from
each other so
people who spoke
the same language
lived together in
different places.

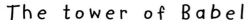

13

Abraham's big family

GENESIS 12, 21

Can you count all the stars in the sky?

God promised Abraham and Sarah a great big family with more children and grandchildren than you can count: just like the stars in the sky. They would all be God's friends, part of God's special people who would love him as he loved them.

Abraham and Sarah had a son called Isaac, the first of many to be part of their big family.

Esau and Jacob

GENESIS 25

Isaac grew up to have two sons of his
own, boys called Esau and Jacob.

One day Esau came home to the wonderful
smell of Jacob's cooking.

'Let me have some of that and you can have
anything you want!' he said.

'Will you trade with me our father's blessing?
Will you give up your right to be the first son?'

'Done!' said Esau, as he started to eat.

Jacob tricks his father

GENESIS 27

Isaac was old and his eyes too weak to see.

'Esau, my son, go hunting for me. When you return, I will bless you as my oldest son.'

While Esau was gone, Jacob dressed in Esau's smelly clothes and took Isaac his favourite meal.

'You smell like Esau and you feel like Esau... but are you really my oldest son?' asked his father.

'Yes I am' Jacob answered.

'Come here and I will bless you.'

When Esau came home, he and his father were angry because they both knew that Jacob had tricked them.

Jacob's favourite son

GENESIS 37, 39 - 50

Jacob married and had lots of children. But Jacob loved his son, Joseph, best of all.

He gave Joseph a beautiful coloured coat, but although Joseph was very happy, his brothers were grumpy and jealous.

Then Joseph had strange dreams. In every one of them, Joseph was very important, and his brothers were bowing down before him.

His brothers were very unhappy.

Soon they were not his friends at all.

21

Sold to be a slave

GENESIS 37, 39

Joseph's brothers watched and waited.

They waited until Joseph was far from home. First the brothers took away his special coat and then they threw Joseph into a deep pit. When traders passed by, they sold Joseph to be a slave in Egypt.

Poor, poor Joseph. He had never worked so hard in his life – until they put him in prison for something he didn't even do!

The King of Egypt

GENESIS 40 - 41

Being a slave was bad but being in prison was worse.

Then the King's baker and cupbearer dreamed strange dreams. Joseph helped them both to understand what their dreams meant so that, much later, when the King also dreamed strange dreams, he called for Joseph to help him.

Then the King was so pleased with Joseph that he made him a great man in the land of Egypt, taking charge of all the grain that grew so that everyone would have enough food to eat.

A very happy family

GENESIS 42 - 47

Jacob and his family were very hungry. They knew there was food in Egypt. They did not know that Joseph was there and ready to help them.

So when they travelled to Egypt to buy food, they were all very happy to find that God had been looking after them all along.

There was Joseph, a very important man, just as in his dreams, ready to forgive his brothers, and very happy to see his father again.

The whole family came to live in Egypt.

Moses and the princess

EXODUS 2

The Egyptians called Joseph's family the Hebrews. They grew in number until the new king of Egypt decided to make the Hebrews his slaves. Then the king decided to kill all their baby boys!

Miriam's mother made a basket and hid Miriam's baby brother inside it beside the River Nile.

Miriam watched the princess find the baby. She saw that God would take care of him so that baby Moses would grow up safe and strong.

The king says 'No!'

Exodus 3 - 12

When Moses was a man, God spoke to him.

'The King of Egypt is being cruel to my people. Tell him to let my people go.'

'My God, the God of all the earth, says, "Let my people go!"' said Moses to the King.

But the King would not let them go. Instead he made their work harder. He treated them even worse than before.

So there were ten terrible plagues in Egypt. Then the King told Moses to take God's people and go!

Escape from Egypt

Exodus 13 - 14

God led thousands upon thousands of his people to the Red Sea.
But when the King realised that all his slaves had gone, he sent
soldiers in chariots to bring them back. Now there were soldiers

behind them and the Red Sea in front of them.

'Trust God!' Moses told the people. The sea parted and a path opened up in front of them; and God's people crossed over to the other side. God's people were free at last.

Gideon's fleece

JUDGES 6

Gideon was not clever or very brave. So when God asked him to lead an army against the cruel Midianites, he shook his head.

'You can't want me,' he said to God. 'I will leave this woolly fleece outside tonight. If it is wet but the ground is dry, then I will know.'

The next morning the fleece was very wet and the ground was completely dry.

'I need to be really sure,' said Gideon. 'Let the fleece be dry while the ground is wet. Then I will know.'

The dew covered the ground next morning but the fleece was completely dry.

Gideon knew that God really had chosen him to lead the army.

A boy called Samuel

I SAMUEL 3

Hannah had a very special little boy called Samuel. He was learning how to serve God with Eli the priest.

One night, after he had gone to bed, he heard someone calling his name. Samuel went to Eli.

'Here I am,' said Samuel. 'You called me.' But Eli sent him away. He had not called Samuel.

A while later Samuel heard the voice calling him again. But when Samuel went again to Eli, the priest sent him back to his bed.

When it happened a third time, Eli sat up and scratched his head. Now he knew who was calling Samuel.

'Say, "Speak Lord, I am listening" when the voice calls again,' said Eli.

Samuel answered as Eli had told him. It was the beginning of Samuel learning to listen to God. He grew up to be a very special prophet who helped God's people.

David and the giant

I SAMUEL 17

Goliath was big and strong and scary. Goliath liked to make people afraid of him. The great King Saul was afraid of him. All the soldiers in Saul's army were afraid of him.

David was not big or strong but David knew God. David knew God could help him stop Goliath from being a bully.

God did help David. All Goliath's friends ran away too. Then King Saul and his army were no longer afraid.

39

Elijah and the ravens

I KINGS 17

There were good Kings and there were bad Kings. King Ahab was a very bad King.

'No more rain will fall until you remember how to be a good King again,' said Elijah the prophet. 'Love the true and living God, lead his people well and rain will fall once more on the land.'

God sent Elijah to a little burbling brook where he could find water. God sent ravens with food to feed Elijah. God took care of Elijah because he had taken the message to the very bad King.

One more drop of oil

1 KINGS 17

The earth was dry. The sun was hot. The water in the brook had dried up.

'Go to Zarephath,' God told Elijah. 'I have told a widow there to share her food with you.'

Elijah found the widow who used her last drop of oil and her last handful of flour to make some bread to share with him. And each time she went again to the jar and the jug, God provided enough flour and another drop of oil to bake more bread.

Washing in the river

2 KINGS 5

Naaman suffered from leprosy, a horrible skin disease.

'If only he would visit the prophet Elisha,' the servant girl told his wife. 'God would be kind and heal my master.'

Naaman did go to visit Elisha.

'Wash seven times in the River Jordan and God will heal you,' said Elisha. But Naaman was a great man. He did not want to wash in the dirty river.

'If the prophet had told you to do something hard, you would have done it. Why not try this?' said his servant.

Naaman washed seven times in the River Jordan and his skin was healed as Elisha had promised. Naaman was amazed.

'Now I know there is no other God than here in Israel,' said Naaman.

Jonah and the big fish

JONAH 1 -3

Jonah boarded a ship and hid below deck. Jonah was God's prophet but he was running away from God! God wanted him to take a message to the people of Nineveh – and he didn't want to go!

Soon a storm blew up, rocking and tipping the ship... and all the sailors were terrified. Jonah knew it was his fault. He told the sailors to throw him into the sea!

And God sent a big fish to catch Jonah. Inside the belly of the fish, Jonah prayed.

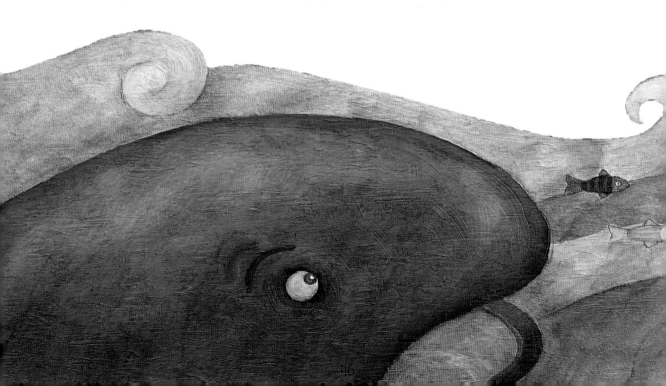

'I'm sorry...' said Jonah.

The big fish spat Jonah on to a sandy shore. Jonah took God's message to Nineveh and the people said sorry too. And because God is kind and forgiving, he forgave them.

Daniel and the lions

DANIEL 6

Daniel loved God and prayed three times every day.

The King made a law that said, 'Pray to me or be thrown to the lions!'

But Daniel still loved God and prayed to him. So Daniel was thrown to the lions...

Daniel loved God and God looked after him. The King set Daniel free and told everyone to worship Daniel's God instead – because God really was amazing and wonderful and had the power to save.

Mary and the angel

LUKE 1

Mary lived in the little village of Nazareth. She was going to marry Joseph, the carpenter.

Then one day, God sent the angel Gabriel to Mary with a message.

'Don't be afraid, Mary. God has chosen you to be the mother of his Son.'

'But how can this happen?' Mary asked. 'I have no husband yet.'

'The child will be the Son of God and you will call him Jesus,' said the angel.

Mary loved God. She was ready to be the mother of this special baby.

50

Mary and Elizabeth

Luke 1

After the angel had come to see her, Mary was so excited she went to share the news with her cousin Elizabeth.

Elizabeth had been very old before she found she was expecting a baby. And as soon as she saw Mary, she knew that God had blessed her too. Together they thanked and praised God.

'You have been so good to me,' Mary said to God. 'You are great and mighty but you love someone like me. You are wise and wonderful but you help us and make us happy.'

Joseph the carpenter

MATTHEW 1

Joseph was a good, kind man.

Mary told Joseph about the angel's news. But when Mary told him that she was going to have a baby, Joseph didn't know what to say! He was afraid people would say unkind things

about her. He knew her baby was not his baby.

Then one night God's angel spoke to him too in a dream.

'Don't be afraid, Joseph,' said the angel. 'Mary's baby will be called Jesus because he will save his people from their sins. Marry her and take care of her and God's Son.'

The journey to Bethlehem

LUKE 2

When Mary's baby was
due to be born, the Roman
emperor, Caesar Augustus,

made everyone go to the home town of their family to be counted.

Joseph took Mary to Bethlehem because he came from the family of the great King David who had lived there hundreds of years before.

It was a long way to Bethlehem. It was a very long way if you were expecting a baby.

No room at the inn

LUKE 2

Mary and Joseph walked for many days. But they were not the only people to be travelling to Bethlehem. Many other families had come to be counted too.

When they arrived at the little town in the hills, they tried to find a place where Mary could rest. But people shook their heads.

'No room! No room!' said one innkeeper after another.

The first Christmas

LUKE 2

At last Mary and Joseph found a place to stay.

Mary knew her baby was coming. Joseph helped to make her comfortable and, on that starry night, Mary's baby Son was born.

She made a bed for her first child in the manger because there was no room for them in the inn.

Mary remembered the message of the angel months before and she called him Jesus.

Shepherds on the hillside

LUKE 2

Out on the hills that night, shepherds were looking after their sheep. Suddenly they were dazzled by a bright and shining light – an angel bringing news of the birth of the baby Jesus!

'You will find the baby in Bethlehem, lying in a manger,' said the angel. Then more angels filled the starry sky. 'Glory to God!' they sang. 'Peace and joy to all the world!'

The shepherds hurried to Bethlehem with the music of the angels ringing in their ears.

The baby Jesus

LUKE 2

When the shepherds found Mary and Joseph, they knelt beside the manger.

Here was the baby the angel had told them about. Here was Jesus, God's own Son.

First they told Mary and Joseph about the angels. Then they told everyone about what they'd seen and heard on that first Christmas night.

Wise men in the east

MATTHEW 2

Far away in the east, a bright and special star shone in the night sky.

Wise men who studied the stars believed it was a sign that a new King had been born.

'We must travel to find him,' said one.

'We must take special gifts,' said another.

'We must worship the baby King,' said another.

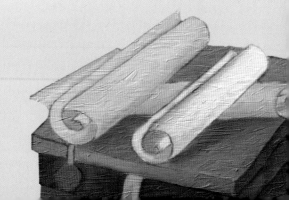

66

Following a star

MATTHEW 2

The wise men prepared for a long journey. They packed treasure chests with gifts fit for a King and set off by night on camels.

Night after night the wise men travelled west, following the star, until they arrived in the city of Jerusalem.

   Expecting to find a *baby* King in a palace, they went to King
Herod and asked where they might find the newborn King.

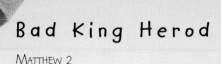

Bad King Herod

MATTHEW 2

King Herod was a jealous king, an angry king.

When the wise men came looking for a baby born to be king of the Jews, he was not happy.

He thought hard. Could there *be* another king? A king who might take his place?

He asked his own wise men whether they knew about this baby king. Herod did not like the answer they gave him.

'The scriptures say he will come from Bethlehem...'

King Herod told the wise men where to look but he had a wicked plan.

'Tell me when you find him,' said King Herod. 'Then I can go to worship him too...'

Gold, frankincense and myrrh

MATTHEW 2

The wise men followed the star to Bethlehem. Many months had passed since they left their homes but now they had found what they were looking for.

The star seemed to stop over a little house and there they found Mary with her little son. The wise men bowed low with their special gifts of gold, frankincense and myrrh.

God told them in a dream not to go back to bad King Herod, so they went home a different way, praising God that they had seen Jesus, God's own Son, the baby King, in Bethlehem.

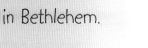

Jesus is baptised

MATTHEW 3

When Jesus was a man he went to find John, Elizabeth's son, who was baptising people in the River Jordan. Jesus wanted to be baptised.

'I cannot baptise you – you should be baptising me!' said John. 'These people come because they are sorry for their sins. You have nothing to be sorry about.'

But Jesus wanted to be washed clean in the water. God was pleased with Jesus.

Now it was time to tell everyone all he knew about God, his Father.

Jesus chooses friends

Luke 5:1-11, 6:12-16

One day Jesus asked Simon Peter to take him out fishing.

'We didn't catch a single fish last night,' Simon Peter told him. 'But I'll take you out now, if you like.'

Simon Peter and his brother Andrew caught hundreds of fish that day. James and John had to help them.

'Come with me,' Jesus said.

Simon Peter, Andrew, James and John became the first four men who, along with Philip, Bartholomew, Matthew, Thomas, another James, another Simon and two men called Judas, were known as friends of Jesus, his disciples.

A hole in the roof

MARK 2

People started listening to Jesus. They knew he was special.

Four men carried their friend on his mat to see him. Their friend couldn't walk and they hoped that Jesus might help him. But the house was very crowded. So they climbed up to the roof – and made a hole so that they could lower their friend down!

That day Jesus healed the man so he could carry his own mat and walk home. It was a miracle.

God loves you!

MATTHEW 6

'God loves you,' said Jesus. 'God who feeds the birds will make sure you have enough to eat. God who makes the flowers beautiful will make sure you have clothes to wear.'

The people did not know that God was good and kind and caring. They did not know that God was like a Father who loved them and cared about them before Jesus came to tell them.

Jesus calms a storm

MARK 4

Many times Jesus spent whole days telling people about God and healing people who were ill.

One day he was so tired that he fell asleep as soon as he got into the boat that took him across the Sea of Galilee.

At first the little boat rocked gently on the waves. But then a sudden storm blew up and the boat lurched up and down dangerously. Jesus stayed sleeping but his friends were very afraid. They woke Jesus and called for his help.

Jesus stood up and spoke to the wind and the waves. Suddenly the wind stopped howling and the sea was still again.

'You don't need to be afraid,' said Jesus. 'Trust me. I am here.'

Jesus heals a little girl

Luke 8

Jairus had a little daughter. But she was ill, very ill. He went to Jesus for help.

'Please come quickly!' Jairus said. 'It's my little girl – I think she's dying.'

Jesus followed Jairus through the crowds of people. But before they reached his home, someone came to say the little girl had died.

Jesus chased away all the weeping women. He took the girl's hand in his.

'Get up, little girl,' he whispered.

Jairus' daughter opened her eyes. Her parents didn't know whether to laugh or cry. Jesus had healed their only daughter.

84

The boy who shared

MATTHEW 14

People followed Jesus wherever he went.

Jesus cared about the mums and dads. He cared about the children.

One day a huge crowd had been with Jesus all day – thousands of people were there – and they were hungry and far from home.

'How can we feed these people?' Jesus said to his friends. 'We must take care of them.'

Andrew brought a boy to Jesus who offered to share his picnic lunch. Jesus said thank you to the boy and thank you to God. Then he shared it with his friends who shared it with the people. And EVERYONE had enough to eat. It was a miracle!

The story of the kind man

Luke 10

A man once came to Jesus and asked, 'I know I must love God and I know I must love other people as much as I love myself. But what does that really mean? Must I love everyone?'

So Jesus told a story.

'A man was attacked as he travelled from Jerusalem to Jericho and left to die by the side of the road. Two very religious men came along the road. Both men crossed over so they didn't come too close and went on their way.

'Later a Samaritan came along. He stopped, treated the man's wounds and helped him on to his own donkey. He took him to an inn and took care of him.'

The man who had asked the question knew the answer now. The Samaritan did the right thing. Jesus wants us to be ready to help anyone who needs us.

The story of the lost sheep

Luke 15

Jesus told another story about how much God loves us.

'Imagine you are a farmer with 100 sheep. You take good care of them. But then one goes missing. Do you forget about that sheep? No, you look in ditches and in hedges. You look in dark stony places in case your sheep is hurt and needs you. You don't rest until you have found your lost sheep and can bring it back safely.

'God is just like that. So if one loses his way, he tries to help them back to the right way. God loves all the people he has made.'

Jesus heals a blind man

MARK:10

Bartimaeus could hear a crowd of people but he could not see
Jesus. Instead he heard people talking about him – and he knew
how Jesus had helped others.

'Jesus!' he called out. 'Help me, please!'

'Sshhh,' said some of the people in the crowd. But this made
Bartimaeus call louder still!

'Jesus! I am over here!'

Jesus stopped. 'What do you want me to do for you?' he asked.

'I just want to see!' Bartimaeus answered.

'Then you will see,' Jesus told him.

Bartimaeus looked for the first time into the kind face of Jesus,
the man who had given him his sight.

He was so happy, he followed Jesus
wherever he went.

The man who climbed a tree

LUKE 19

When Jesus went to Jericho, he met a man who had no friends – and Jesus changed his life.

Everybody knew Zacchaeus but nobody liked him. Zacchaeus worked as a tax collector for the Romans – and he was a cheat who had become a very rich man.

Zacchaeus wanted very much to meet Jesus but he was so small that he had to climb a tree to see him. Then he looked down at Jesus as Jesus looked up at him!

'Come down, Zacchaeus!' said Jesus. 'I'd like to come to your house today.'

Zacchaeus had never been so happy! 'I will give half my money to the poor,' he told people. 'And if I have cheated anyone, I will pay them back four times what I owe them!'

Zacchaeus was a changed man now Jesus was his friend.

Mary, Martha and Lazarus

JOHN 11

Jesus often visited his friend
Lazarus and his two sisters. But
one day he received a message
that Lazarus was very ill.

By the time Jesus reached their
house, Lazarus had died.
Mary was inside the house,
weeping. Martha went to meet Jesus.

'I wish you had been here,' she said. 'Then I know he would not
have died.'

'Do you trust me, Martha?' asked Jesus. 'Come with me to the tomb
where you have buried your brother.'

Martha, Mary and all their friends went to the tomb. Then Jesus
prayed and called Lazarus out of the tomb.

Lazarus came out – still in his grave clothes – and all
who watched were amazed. Jesus had brought Lazarus
back from the grave.

Jesus rides a donkey

MARK 11

It was time to go to Jerusalem for the Passover festival. Jesus' friends were watching and waiting as he came riding on a little donkey.

'Look! Here's Jesus!' they said, making a soft path for the donkey's feet.

'Hooray for Jesus, our king!' shouted others, waving palm branches and cheering.

But not everyone was happy. Some of the religious leaders were cross. Why were people treating Jesus this way? They didn't like it at all.

Love one another

JOHN 13

It was time to eat supper together. But Jesus was on his knees preparing to wash the feet of all his friends.

'You are surely not going to wash my feet, too,' Peter asked Jesus.

'Let me do this if you are my friend, Peter. I want to show you that no one is greater than anyone else. Be kind to each other. Take care of each other. Love one another in the same way that I have loved you.'

The last supper

Jesus knew that Judas didn't want to be his friend any more. Soon Judas would leave the room and those religious men would be giving him thirty silver coins. Some very sad things were about to happen.

'This bread we share is like my body,' said Jesus. 'Soon it will be broken. This cup of wine is like my blood,' said Jesus. 'Soon it will be spilled.

His friends did not understand what Jesus meant. But Judas was already on his way to tell the religious men where they could find Jesus.

Praying in the garden

LUKE 22

After supper, Jesus went to a garden to pray. The moonlight shone on the olive trees. Jesus asked his friends to keep watch.

Then Jesus prayed, asking God to help him be brave. He knew some very bad things were going to happen.

Then Jesus found that his friends had fallen asleep!

Suddenly men armed with swords and clubs were coming through the trees. And there, leading them, was Judas, one of the twelve men Jesus had trusted.

Jesus on trial

LUKE 22

Jesus was arrested and marched off. All the disciples
were so frightened they ran away. But Peter followed the
men to a courtyard to see what would happen to Jesus.

'Aren't you a friend of Jesus?' said someone there.

'Weren't you with him?' said another.

'You even have the same accent!' said a third.

'No, No, NO!' said Peter.

'I don't know him at all. Jesus is not my friend!'

Then Peter realised what a terrible thing he had done.

The angry crowd

Luke 23

Pontius Pilate, the Roman governor, was worried. Why had they brought this kind, gentle man to him?

Pilate knew Jesus had done nothing wrong. But he saw that the religious leaders wanted him to die. He hoped the crowd would help him.

'What shall I do with Jesus?' Pilate asked them.

'Crucify him!' they shouted. 'Put him on a cross to die!'

Pilate wanted nothing more to do with this. He washed his hands and told his soldiers to take Jesus away.

108

The heavy cross

Luke 23

The soldiers made fun of Jesus. They put a crown made of sharp thorns on his head. Then they made him carry a large piece of wood to a hill where there were other crosses. It was very heavy; it hurt his shoulders.

It was a long walk to the hill outside the city walls. When Jesus fell down, the soldiers hit him. Then they made a man from the crowd pick up the wood and carry it the rest of the way.

Jesus is crucified

LUKE 23

On the hillside, Jesus was nailed to the piece of wood between two thieves.

'If you are the man who works miracles – save yourself!' called the man on the cross on one side of Jesus.

'Leave him alone,' said the man on the other cross. 'He doesn't deserve to die as we do.'

John, one of Jesus' friends, comforted Mary, his mother.

'Look after my mother, John!' said Jesus. Then to his mother, Jesus said, 'Treat John as your son now.'

A little while later, Jesus died.

Buried in a rock tomb

Luke 23

Jesus died on a Friday afternoon. All Jesus' friends were very, very sad.

One of them, a friend called Joseph, asked Pontius Pilate if he could bury Jesus' body in his own rock tomb. They took Jesus down from the cross and carried his body to the garden where the tomb was.

Some of the women followed, weeping, and saw the place where Jesus was buried. They watched as a huge stone door was rolled across the entrance.

Jesus is alive!

LUKE 24

Everyone rested on Saturday but, early on Sunday morning, Mary Magdalene and some other friends went to the garden with flowers and herbs.

They had a big surprise! The heavy stone door had been rolled away from the entrance and some angels told them: 'Jesus is not here. He is no longer dead – Jesus is alive!'

Mary did not understand how this could be but a little while later Jesus came into the garden – and she saw Jesus for herself!

Jesus meets his friends

JOHN 20

Mary was not the only person to see Jesus.

Ten of the disciples were so afraid that they would also be arrested and taken away that they were locked inside a room together.

Suddenly Jesus came and stood among them. They knew that he had died. It was not a mistake. But now they saw that he was very much alive. Jesus even had something to eat and drink with them.

Thomas believes

JOHN 20

Thomas had not been there when Jesus came to see the other disciples. The others told him what had happened but he shook his head.

'Unless I see him for myself, and touch the wounds in his body, I cannot believe Jesus is alive,' he said.

Then Jesus came again into the locked room. 'Hello, Thomas,' he said. 'Come and put your fingers in these wounds in my hands and in my side. See for yourself that it is really me!'

Thomas fell to his knees. He saw for himself that Jesus was alive. And he did believe that he had been dead – and God had raised him to life again.

Breakfast on the beach

John 21

One night, seven of the disciples went fishing.

'Have you caught any fish?' someone called.

'None at all!' Peter shouted back.

'Try again,' said the man on the beach.

When the net filled with silvery fishes, Peter knew it was Jesus. He jumped into the water to get to him faster.

The men joined Jesus for breakfast on the beach. Jesus knew that Peter was sad because he was remembering the day when he had told people that he didn't know Jesus and he was not his friend.

Peter loved Jesus. He was his best friend. After they had talked, Peter knew Jesus had forgiven him.

The Holy Spirit comes

ACTS 2

Jesus stayed with his friends for a little while and then he went back to God in Heaven.

'God will soon send the Holy Spirit to help you. It will feel as if I am there with you all the time. You will never feel alone,' said Jesus.

On the day of Pentecost the Holy Spirit came to them

like tongues of fire and like a very strong wind.

Afterwards they felt wonderful! It felt as if they could do anything because now they had the power to do things that were kind and good and brave. And because they did those things, people all over the world know about Jesus today and are his friends too.

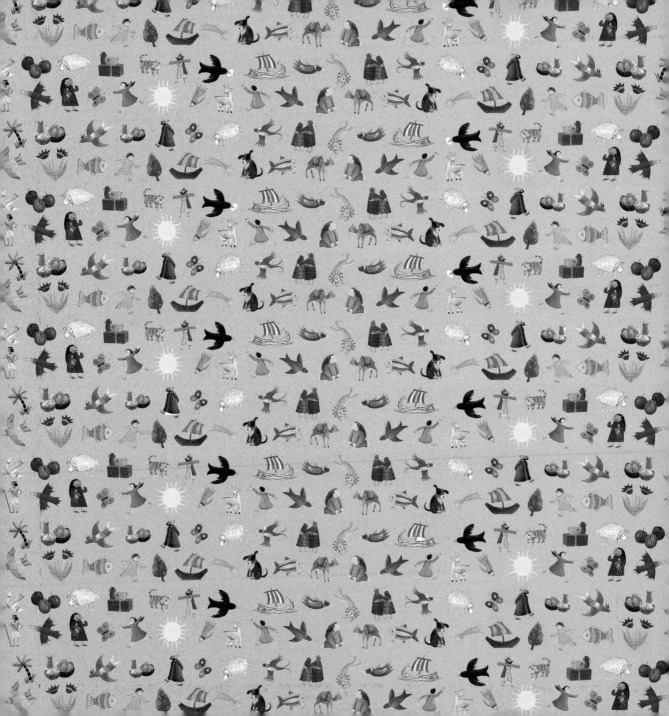